THIS DICTIONARY
and every word in it, from A to Z,
BELONGS TO:

_____

quiet · umbrella · buzz · wagon · yellow · pirate · table · refrigerator · sea · early · yet · hop

very · vacation · up · lion · kite · ostrich · tongue · cow · ouch · kitchen · juice · whack · gasoline · lion · yell · breakfast · owl · newspaper · firefly · ivy · accident

X-ray · zyxuzpf · ice cream · xanthophyll · junkyard · Indian · ivy · junkyard · quart · moon · wag · Halloween · television · shadow · ax · ice skates · hop · noodle · freeze · Oobooglunk · vaccination · wait · key · rabbit · ear · tricycle · whale · joke · balloon · knife · magic · X-ray · valentine · nine · hard · net · raincoat · jet · kite · lasso · sandwich · jelly · mustard · cheese · yard · alphabet · yawn

The Cat in the Hat
Beginner Book
DICTIONARY

**by the Cat himself
and
P.D. Eastman**

BEGINNER BOOKS
A Division of Random House, Inc.

This title was originally cataloged by the Library of Congress as follows:
Seuss, Dr.   The cat in the hat dictionary, by the Cat himself and P. D. Eastman.
(New York) Beginner Books (1964).   133 p.   col. illus.   29 cm.
1. Picture dictionaries, English—Juvenile literature.   I. Eastman, Philip D., joint author.
II Title.   PE1629.G4.   64—11457.
ISBN: 0-394-81009-0 (trade) ; 0-394-91009-5 (lib. bdg.)

Manufactured in the United States of America
70 69 68 67 66 65 64

This dictionary has a serious purpose.

There is nothing more serious than helping a child learn how to read.

But the Editors of Beginner Books, who put this dictionary together, decided they could be serious...and still avoid being stuffy.

So they made this book of words just as funny as they could make it.

It's full of ridiculous alligators, foolish bears and giraffes' uncles, all racing around and getting involved in nonsensical adventures.

The average child, we've discovered, seems to like things just that way. And that is fine. It helps us to focus the child's attention on the serious job we're trying to accomplish...to make him recognize, remember, *and really enjoy* a basic elementary vocabulary of 1350 words.

* * *

We offer you no rules on how to use this book with your children.

Maybe, the first time around, you'll want to read it to them.

The second time around, they may read some of it to *you*.

Dr. Seuss

A a

Aaron

Aaron is an alligator.

above

Aaron above the clouds

about

Aaron is about to go up.

accident

Accident. Poor Aaron!

across

Abigail going across

add

Abigail is adding.

afraid

Abigail is afraid.

after

A mouse after a cat

again

Aaron is up again.

ah

Say "ah."

ahead

The cat is ahead of the mouse.

3

airplane

Airplanes

along

"Come along."

alike

All alike

alphabet

alone

All alone

always

Aaron is
always having accidents.

4

American

American Indian

angry

An angry animal

another

Another angry animal

answer

Answer it! Answer it!

ant

Ants in pants

any

Are there any more ants anywhere around?

apple

Arms full of apples

5

arrow

aunt

Abigail's Aunt Ada

ask

Abigail asking for an apple

auto

Aunt Ada's auto

asleep

Aaron asleep

Aaron awake

away

Away goes Aunt Ada.

ax

6

B b

baby

bad

back

A baby on an animal's back

7

A bad baby

bag
baggage

bake

A baker baking bread

ball

Baseball Football

balloon

Baby likes balloons.

banana

Baby likes bananas.

band

bank

A piggy bank

8

barber

Aaron at the barber's

bark

Dogs do it.

barn

basket

A baby in a basket

bat

Aunt Ada batting

bath

Bathtub   Shower bath

bear

bell

Ringing bells

bed

A bear in bed in his bedroom

belt

A bear with a belt

bee

Bees after a bear

beside

A bear beside a tree

behind

A bear behind a tree

between

A bear between trees

bicycle

Aunt Ada's bike

big

Big   Bigger   Biggest

bird

birthday

A bird's birthday cake

bit

He bit a big bite.

black

A blackbird at a blackboard

block

blow

A breeze is blowing.

blue

body

Bones in a body

book

A book about birds

boot

Bird boots

bottle

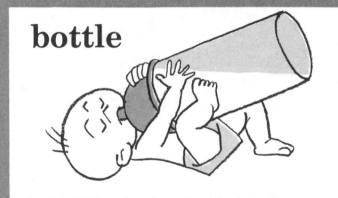

bowl

Bananas in a bowl

12

box

Bananas in a box

boy

Boy bear   Girl bear

break

Breaking the bank

breakfast

Breakfast in bed

breathe

Breathe in.   Breathe out.

brick

Bricks

bridge

A baby in a boat in a brook
under a bridge

13

bright

Bright light

brother

A bear and his brother

bring

"Bring me a balloon, boy."

brush

A bear brushing

broom

bubble

Bubble gum

build

Builders building a building

bump

burn

I burned it.

bus

butter

A butterfly on the butter

button

Big blue buttons

buzz

Bees buzz by.

cactus

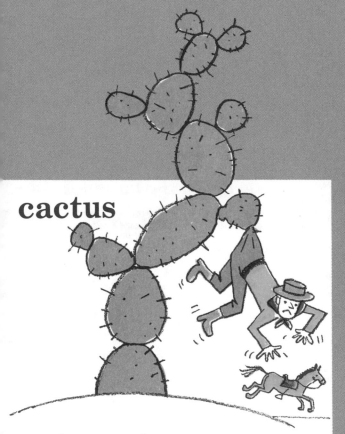

Cowboy caught on a cactus

cage

An animal in a cage

calf

A cow's child

call

"HERE, CAMEL, CAMEL, CAMEL."

Aunt Ada calling her camel

16

camera

candle

camp

Campfire

candy

Chocolate candy

cap

We all have caps.

can

"I can't open this can! Can you?"

car

Car   Cart

17

castle

cent

Five cents make a nickel.

chair

Bears in chairs

catch

Catching the ball

chase

Chasing a fly

ceiling

A fly on the ceiling

cheese

"I love it."

chicken

Chicken   Chicks

child

Child   Children

chimney

Santa Claus comes down it.

chin

Christmas

Merry Christmas

church

circle

All in a circle

19

city

Village   Town   City

clean

Cleaning the city

climb

Climbers climbing

clock

Alarm clock   Cuckoo clock

clothes

Clothes   Clothesline   Clothespins

clown

Circus clown

coat

20

Aunt Ada's fur coat

cold

come

"Come!"   He came.

colors

cook

A cook cooking a cookie

comb

corn

Corn   Popcorn

corner

A mouse in a corner

cow

Cow   Calf   Bull

could

He could.   He couldn't.

crack

A crack in the mirror

count

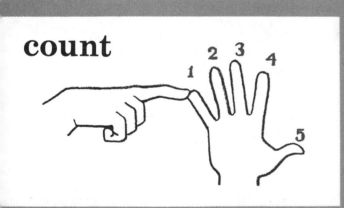

crash

Aaron crashed again.

country

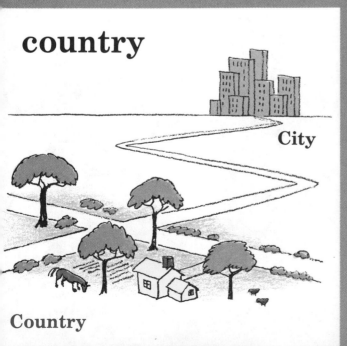

City

Country

crayon

Baby likes crayons.

crow

crowd

A crowd of crows

crown

cry

Babies do it.

cup

Cup and saucer

cut

Aaron cutting

D d

dad

"My daddy is dancing with Aaron."

deep

dark

Dark night   Light day   24   Down deep

dentist

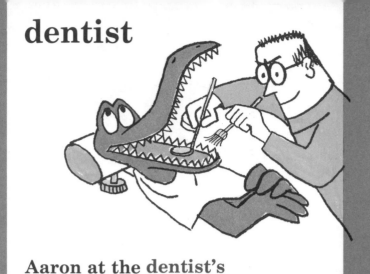

Aaron at the dentist's

dinner

Cooking dinner

dinosaur

dishes

Dirty dishes

dive

Aunt Ada diving

do

The "do" words

does

did

doing

doesn't

don't

done

doctor

Dog doctor

25

doll

A dollar doll

down

up

down

door

"Close that door."

dot

Dots

dozen

A dozen doughnuts   Twelve

draw

Drawing a duck

dream

Dreaming about dresses

drink

A deer drinking

drip

Drops are dripping.

drum

dry

Drying her hair

dump

dust

E e

ear

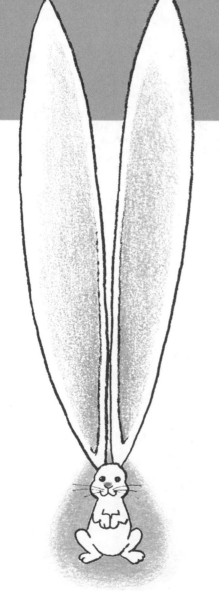

Big ears

early

An early bird

east

28 **A bird going east**

eat

Eating eight eggs

electric

Electric shaver

elephant

eleven

He ate eleven.

empty

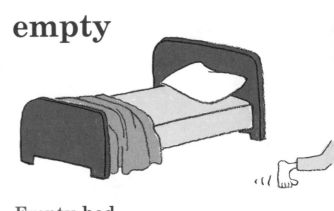

Empty bed

end

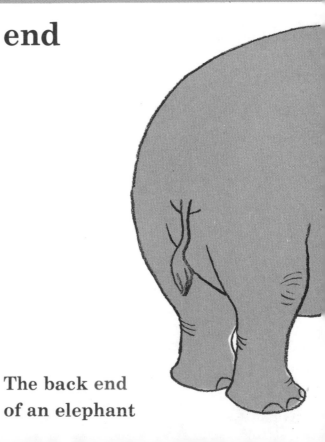

The back end of an elephant

29

entrance

exercise

Aunt Ada exercising

Eskimo

explode

eye

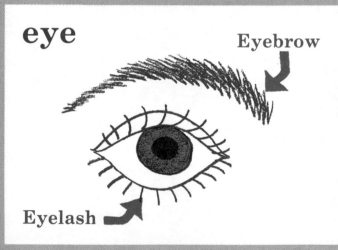

Eyebrow

Eyelash

every

The "every" words

everyone

everybody

everything

everywhere

eyeglasses

F f

fairy

face

fall

"Wash your face."

31

The fairy fell on her face.

family

A large family

fan

Electric fan

far

The star is far away.

farm

A farmer farming on a farm

fast

Fast   **Faster**   **Fastest**

fat

A fat bear   **A thin bear**

father

"That is my father."

feather

Fine feathers

feed

Feeding spinach to the baby

feel

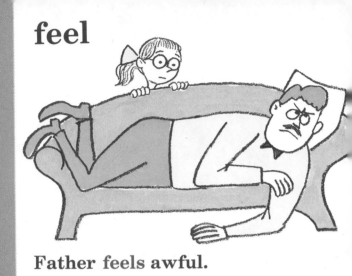

Father feels awful.

feet

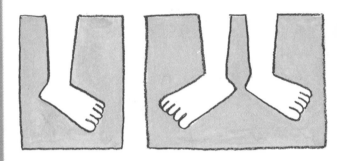

Foot   Feet

fence

33

Feet on a fence

few

A few fish

A lot of fish

finger

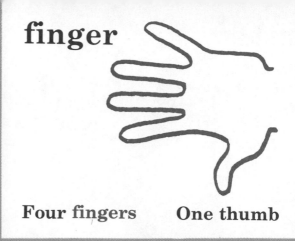

Four fingers   One thumb

fight

fill

"Fill it full."

fire

Firemen on a fire engine going to a fire

firefly

find

Finding a nickel

first

First   Second   Third

five

Five pelicans

fix

"Can you fix it, Father?"

flag

Flags on a boat

flashlight

flat

Flat tire

float

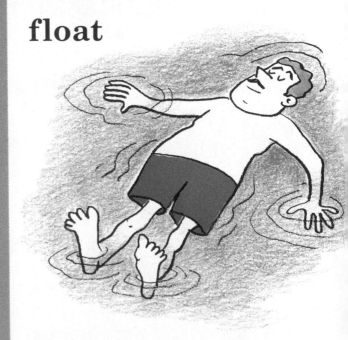

Father floating

35

floor

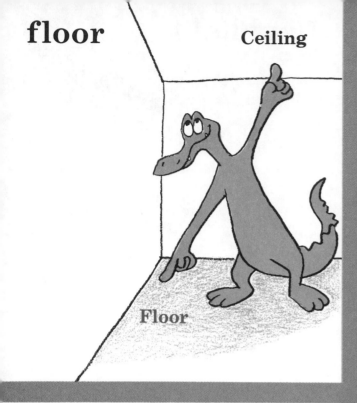

Ceiling

Floor

follow

Follow the leader.

flower

A big flower

food

fly

Aaron is flying again.

36

fork

Knife

Fork

found

He **found** a fox in the forest.

freeze

"IT'S FREEZING IN HERE."

Food freezer

four

Four foxes

fresh

A **fresh egg**

free

friend

37

Friendly frogs

frown

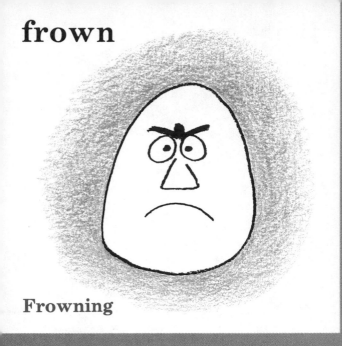

Frowning

fruit

grapes

pear

grapefruit

pineapple

watermelon

lemon

banana

fun

G g

game

A game of cards

garbage

Aunt Ada's garbage

garage

Aunt Ada's garage

garden

Flower garden

39

gargle

A **gargling** bear

gasoline

"**Give** me a **gallon**."

gave

He **gave** him a gallon.

get

"What did you **get** for Christmas? We **got** a bike."

giant

A **great** big man

40

giraffe

glove

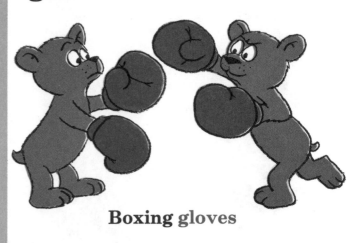

Boxing gloves

go

The **sun** **goes** **down.**
The **sun** is **going** **down.**

glad

Glad   Sad

gone

The **sun** is **gone.**

glass

good

Good dog   Bad dog

41

good-by

grandfather

My father   My grandfather

goose

Goose   Geese

grape

Sour grapes

grass

Goats eat grass.

grade

First grade   Second grade

42

grasshopper

Grasshoppers hopping

gray

grow

"My flowers have grown."

groceries

guess

"Guess who!"

ground

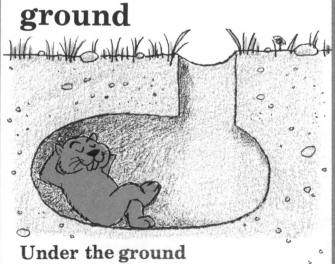

Under the ground

gun

Popgun

H h

hair

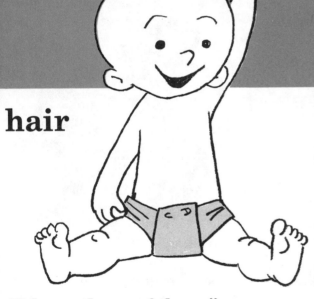

"I have three of them."

hall

half

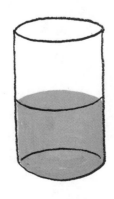

Half full

Halloween

44

ham

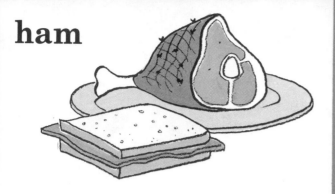

Ham sandwich

hammer

Hammering

hand

Shaking hands

hang

"Hang it on the hanger."

happen

"Everything happens to me."

happy

"Happy birthday to us!"

hard

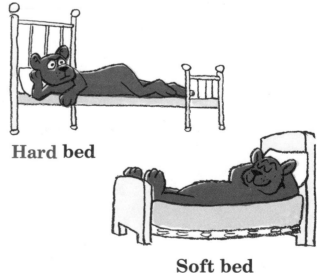

Hard bed

Soft bed

45

hat

His hat   **Her hat**

heart

Heart   **Club**   **Diamond**   **Spade**

hay

Cows eat it.

heavy

head

Aunt Ada on her head

helicopter

hear

He hears with his ears.

46

Aunt Ada's helicopter

hello

help

hen

"My mother is a hen."

here

Hair here   No hair there

hide

Aaron is hiding.

high

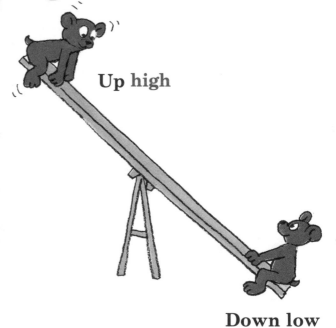

Up high

Down low

hit

Clown hitting clown

hold

Holding the baby

hole

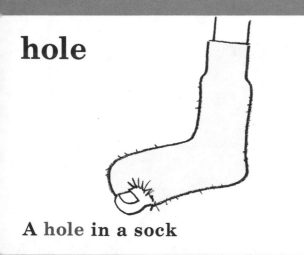

A hole in a sock

holiday

Christmas is a holiday.

hollow

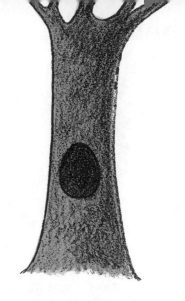

Hollow tree

home

"This is my home."

honey

Bees make it.

48

honk

Geese do it.

horse

hook

Fishhook

hot

A hot horse

hop

Frogs do it.

hour

Hour hand

Minute hand

horn

A goat with three horns

49

house

A horse in a house

hump

One hump

Two humps

hungry

They are hungry.

hunt

Hunting ducks

hurry

"Don't hurry so."

hurt

He hurried and he got hurt.

I i

ice cream

igloo

An Eskimo house

ice skates

inch

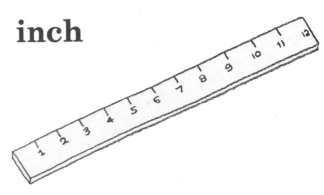

Twelve inches   A foot

51

Indian

An American
Indian

An Indian from India

iron

An Indian ironing his pants
on an island

ink

itch

"I itch."

insect

"I have insects
inside my igloo."

ivy

"I got my itch from -
poison ivy."

Jack

James

Jerry

Joe

jacket

Jack in a jacket

jam

James at the jam jar

jack-o-lantern

Jack's jack-o-lantern

jelly

Jerry in the jelly jar

53

jet

Jerry in his jet

joke

Joe playing a joke on Jack

juice

Jack likes juice.

jump

James jumps over Jack and Joe.

jungle

Jerry in a jungle

junk

Jack, James, Jerry, and Joe in a junk yard

K k

kangaroo

kerchoo

Sneezers do it.

keep

"Keep away from the kangaroo."

key

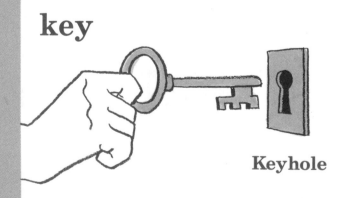

Keyhole

kick

Aunt Ada is a good kicker.

king

kill

Kill that fly.

kiss

Kissed by a king

kind

Two kinds of birds

kite

"Don't fly kites in the kitchen."

kitten

A cat's child

knees

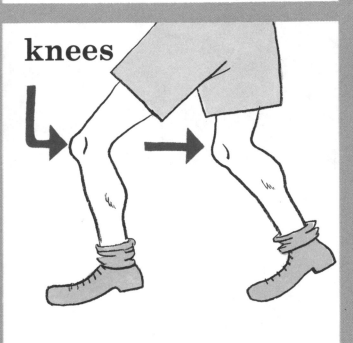

knife

"Don't eat with your knife."

knock

Knocking

know

"I know he is going to fall down."

"I knew it."

57

L l

ladder

A lady on a ladder

lamb

"My child is a lamb."

lake

Lake Minnihaweetonka

land

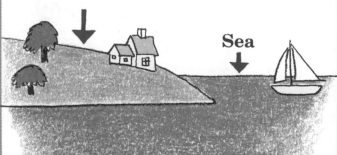

Sea

lap

Sitting on laps

late

Late for school

lasso

laugh

Laughing   **Crying**

last

The last pretzel

lazy

"We all feel lazy."

learn

"He is learning to fly."

leg

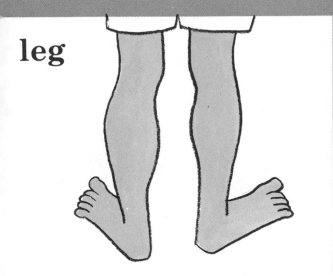

Left leg   Right leg

let

"Let me out of here."

letter

Letter box

library

Books!   Books!   Books!

lick

lie

"Lie down."

He lay down.

lightning

lift

Aaron lifting a lot of lemons

lion

Aunt Ada likes lions.

light

The lighthouse light is lit.

lip

Lips

listen

Listening

lollipops

Baby likes them.

long

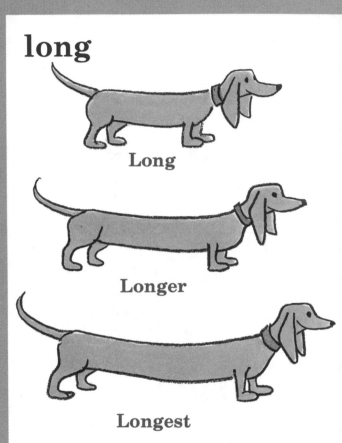

Long

Longer

Longest

little

Little bird   Big bird

log

A frog on a log

62

look

Looking for a lost sock

loose

The goose is loose.

loud

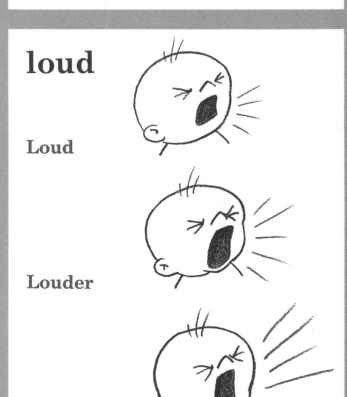

Loud

Louder

Loudest

love

She loves her baby.

luck

Lucky four leaf clover

lump

One lump

lunch

Lunch box

63

M
m

machine

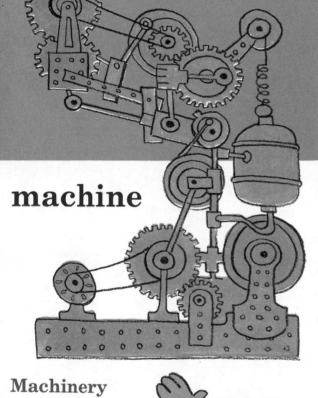

Machinery

magic

made

"I made it all by myself."

64

A magician doing magic

mail

Mailbag   Mailman   Mailbox

map

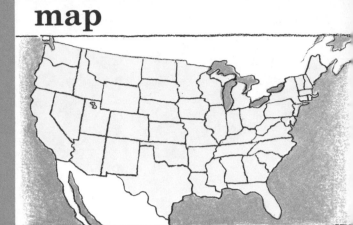

A map of the United States

make

Aaron is making more machines.

marble

A game of marbles

man

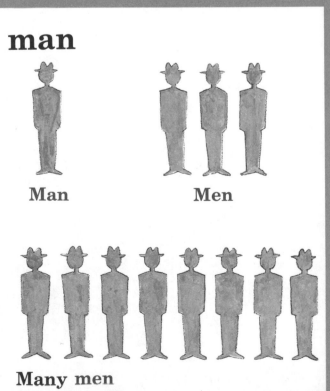

Man   Men

Many men

mask

A moose mask

65

mat

Door mat

match

Be careful.
Little matches make big fires.

may
maybe

He may dive in.
Maybe he will.
He might.　　He might not.

meat
meet

Meeting at the meat market

meow

Cats do it.

merry

Merry-go-round

mess

An awful mess

minute

Five minutes to five

midnight

Midnight is the middle
of the night.

miss

He missed the bus.

million

There are millions of stars.

mitten

"We all have mittens."

67

mix

The cook is mixing eggs and flour.

money

Jack has more money than Joe.

monkey

A monkey with a monkey wrench

month

The twelve months

moo

Cows do it.

They also give milk.

68

moon

Aaron is going there.

morning

"What a beautiful morning!"

mother

"She is the mother of me."

mountain

Mountain   Hill

mouth

Open mouth   Shut mouth

move

Moving to another house

movie

Mr. and Mrs.

Mr. Mouse   Mrs. Mouse

mud

Aunt Ada is stuck in the mud.

music

Making music

must
mustard

"You must not eat
so much mustard."

N n

nail

name

"My name is Tom."

"My name is Oobooglunk."

near

Oobooglunk lives near Nubbglubb.

71

neck

Necktie

never

"He will never get me."

need

"We need a bath."

new

New shoe   Old shoe

nest

newspaper

net

next

"I am next."

night

noise

"Stop that noise."

noodle

Noodle soup

nine

Nine nights

noon

The middle of the day

no

No more left
None
Not a drop

north

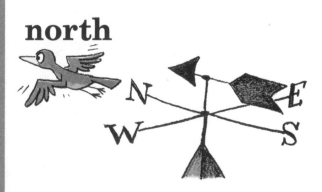

A bird flying north

nose

Little nose   Big nose

nurse

Aaron's nurse

nothing

Nothing at all

now

"It is now four-thirty."

nut

Coconut

numbers

39,570,868

33 $\frac{1}{3}$

100

428

2

65

$\frac{1}{7}$

12

oar

ocean

off

"Oh! I fell off."

office

Father's office

often

"I fall off often."

oil

Oiling the bike

old

An old, old mouse

one

One onion   Only one

open

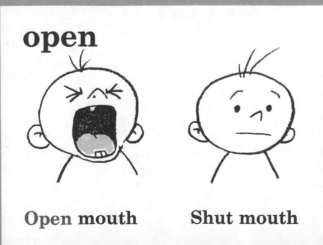

Open mouth   Shut mouth

76

ostrich

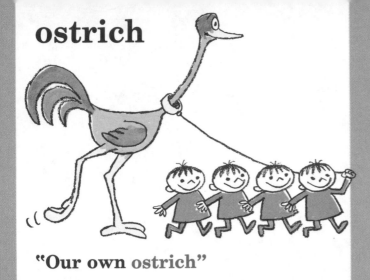

"Our own ostrich"

over

Over a clover

other

One orange is green.
The other orange is orange.

overalls

Overalls on Aaron

ouch

out

Out of the house
Outdoors   Outside

77

owl

"We own our own owl."

P p

pack

Packing his suitcase

paddle

Canoe paddle

package

Carrying packages

page

Books have pages.

pails

palace

"My house"

paint

Painting a picture

pan

A pan full of pancakes

pants

A pair of pants

pajamas

Aaron likes pretty pajamas.

papa

Another name for dear old daddy

79

paper

The paper boy

parachute

parade

A parade in a park

part

A centaur is part man and part horse.

party

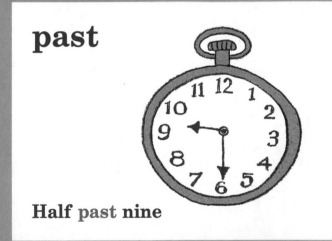

Birthday party

past

Half past nine

pat

Patting the dog

paw

A dog's hand

pedal

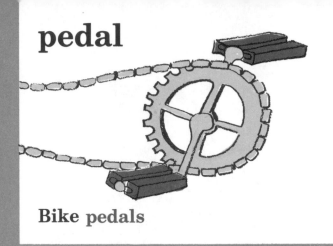

Bike pedals

pay

Paying for the tickets

pen
pencil

A penguin
with a pen and a pencil

people

People   Animals

peanuts

Peanut shells

pepper

Pepper   Salt

pet

Cats and dogs are good pets.

phone

Phoning from a phone booth

phonograph

piano

pick

Picking up after the picnic

pie

A piece of pumpkin pie

pig

A pink pig on a pillow

pin

Safety pin

pinch

Crabs do it.

pirate

pitcher

A pitcher full of jum-jum juice

plant

Planting a jum-jum plant

plate

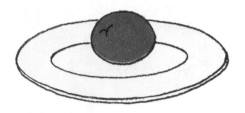

A plum on a plate

play

Playing on the playground

83

please

pole

Pole **vaulting**

pockets

Kangaroos have them.

police

"I am a **police** horse."

point

Pointing

pony

Pony   Pony **cart**

pool

Swimming pool

pop

"My pop is popping popcorn."

porpoise

Happy porpoises

pot

Hot pot

potato

Hot potato

pound

A sixteen-pound baby

pour

Pouring the jum-jum juice

prize

push

Aunt Ada pushing her car

puddle

put

Putting out the cat

pull

"Pull me out of this puddle."

pup
puppy

"This pup is my puppy."

puzzle

Puzzled by a puzzle

Qq

quack

QUACK
QUACK
QUACK
QUACK
QUACK
QUACK

Ducks do it.

quart

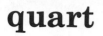

A **quart** of milk

queen

A quart of milk
for the **queen**

question

The queen asked a **question:**
"Is this milk fresh?"
"No, queen. It is old milk,"
answered the milkman.

quick

"Quick," said the queen.
"Take this milk away **quickly**."

quiet

The **quiet** milkman took
the quart away **quietly**.

R r

rabbit

race

A rabbit race
The rabbits are racing.

radio

Hearing news on the radio

IT IS GOING TO RAIN

rain

Rain is raining
on the rabbits.

raincoat

Rabbits racing in raincoats

89

ranch

"I am a cowboy.
I live on a ranch."

rat

read

A rat reading

red

refrigerator

reindeer

"There is a reindeer
in our refrigerator."

90

remember

"I know that bear, but
I can't remember his name."

rest

A long man having
a long rest

ribbon

Hair ribbons

rich

The king is rich.

ride

"We are riding a rhinoceros."

right

Left foot   Right foot

ring

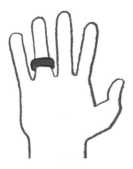

91

ring

Our phone rang.
It is always ringing.

rock

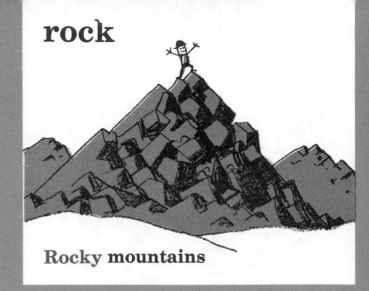

Rocky mountains

river

Ducks on a river

rocket

A rocket
over rocky mountains

road

Ducks on a road

rode
rodeo

The cowboy
rode at the rodeo.

roll

Aunt Ada **rolling**
on **roller** skates

rooster

A hen's husband

roof

Roller skating on the roof

rope

room

"My room is a mess."

rose

**A bunch of roses
for the queen**

93

round

Hoops are round.

rug

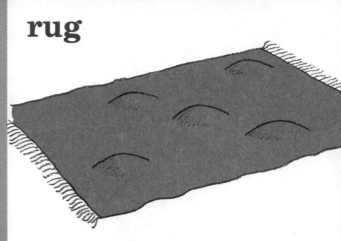

Five robins under a rug

row

Rowing in a rowboat

row

Five robins in a row

rub

Cats like to rub on chairs.

run

The running rhinoceros
ran to Rochester.

S s

sad

A sad, sad dog

saddle

safe

95

"He can't get me. I'm safe."

sail

A **sailor** **sailing**
in a **sailboat**

same

"We look alike.
We look the **same**."

sand

Sandbox

sandwich

A big **sandwich**

sank

"My sailboat **sank**."

save

People **save** money.

Squirrels **save** nuts.

saw

"I see a saw."

saw

"I saw a seesaw."

say

Baby said something.
But what did he say?

scissors

scooter

scratch

Dogs do it.

sea
seal

A seal in the sea

season
There are
four seasons.

Spring

Autumn

Summer

Winter

seeds

Plant them.

They grow.

sell

"He sells hot dogs.
He sold one to me."

send
sent

Mother sent us to bed.

set

A set of books

A TV set

seven

Seven sisters

sew

Seven sisters sewing shirts

sharp

Needles are sharp.

shadow

Aunt Ada's shadow

she

"I am a boy bird.
She is a girl bird."

shake

Shaking paws

sheep

shell

"My house is a shell."

shoot

Shooting an arrow   A good shot

shine

Shoeshine

short

"My shirt is too short."

ship

A big boat

shout

CAN YOU HEAR ME

Shouting

show

Daddy showed his movies.
It was not a good show.

side

Left side　　Right side

Inside　　　　Outside

shut
shutters

Shutting the shutters

sign

Signboards

sick

silly

Making a silly face

sing

Seven sisters
singing songs

skate

A skunk on skates

sky

"We fly in the sky."

sit

The seven sisters sat down.
They are sitting on a seat.

sled

six

Six skunks

sleep

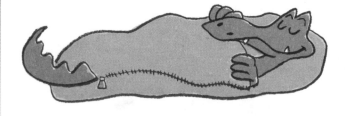

Sleeping in a sleeping bag

103

slide

Sliding

smell

Skunks do.

slow

Slow   Fast

smile

small

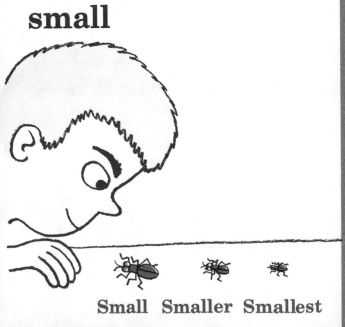

Small Smaller Smallest

smoke

Smoking **chimneys**

104

snack

Eating a **snack** in a shack

sneeze

A snake **sneezing**

sniff

snort

Bulls do it.

snow

Snowflakes

Snowman

Snowball

Snowshoes

Snowshovel

soap

Soapsuds

sock

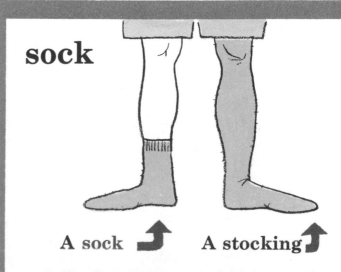

A sock   A stocking

some

somebody

somehow

someone

something

sometimes

somewhere

The "some" words

spider

Spider web

spill

Spilled milk

south

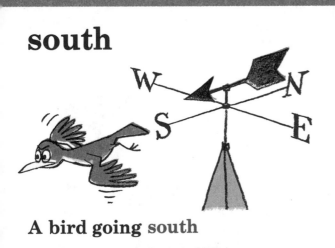

A bird going south

spell

"How do you spell Llewellyn?"

106

spin

A spinning top

splash

Elephants make big ones.

spot

"They call me Spot."

stair

Going down the stairs

stamp

You lick it. You stick it.

stand

Soldiers standing at attention

start

Aunt Ada can't start her car.

107

station

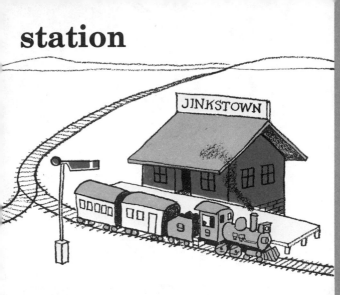

Railroad station

stay

"You stay home.
You can't come along."

steps

Steep steps

stick

Smart dogs fetch sticks.

still

Standing still

sting

Mosquitoes do it.

stone

Rolling stones

stop

Aaron stopped.

story

STORY BOOK

A bedtime story

straight

Straight hair   Curly hair

street

OAK STREET

PINE STREET

string

Kite string

suit

SALE   SALE

KLOPFER'S STORE

Suits in a store

sun

On Sunday it was sunny.
Daddy got a sunburn.

swallow

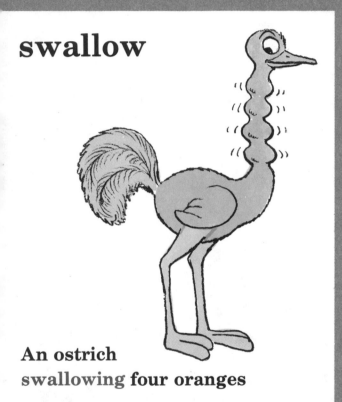

An ostrich
swallowing four oranges

sweaters

sweep

swim

Fish do it.

swing

T t

table

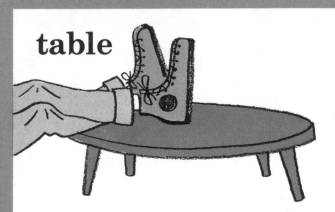

Feet on the table

take

**"Take those feet
off that table."**

tail

A long one

talk

**Everybody talking
Nobody listening**

111

tall

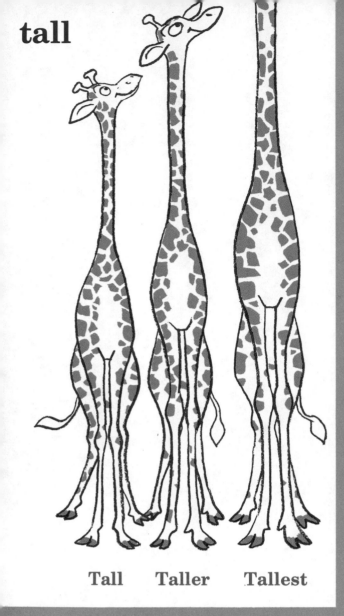

Tall   Taller   Tallest

taste

"This lemon tastes sour."

teach

Their teacher is teaching them to sing.

tame

Tame lion   Lion tamer

telephone

"Hello. Are you there?"

television

thank

"Thanks
for the thirteen tomatoes."

tell

"I will tell you again. I
told you before. NOT SO LOUD!"

thermometer

thing

ten

Ten in a tent

think

A blue thing thinking about
a red thing

thread

throw

"Did you throw this?"

three

Three things

thumb

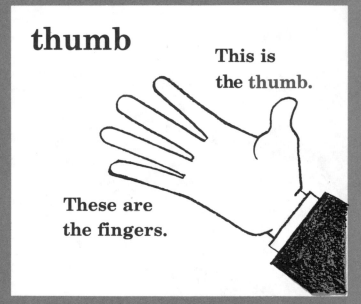

This is
the thumb.

These are
the fingers.

threw

He threw it
through the window.

tie

He tied the tiger tight.

114

time

"The time is now twelve to twelve."

toe

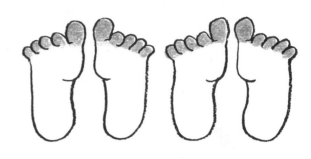

Twenty toes

tired

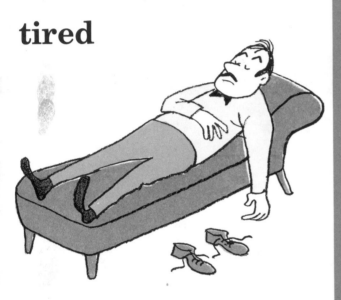

All tired out

tongue

today

Today is the twelfth.

Tomorrow is the thirteenth.

too

Too fat   Too thin

115

tooth

Tooth

Teeth

Toothbrush

tower

**A bear with a towel
on top of a tower**

top

**"There is a green thing
on top of my hat."**

toy

Toy town

towel

A bear with a towel

116

train

Trains run on tracks.

tree

A red thing on a **tree**

truck

A **truck** full of rabbits

trick

My dog does **tricks**.

true

Don't believe him.
It is not **true**.

tricycle

trunk

An elephant's nose

117

try

"I will try to fly."

"I shouldn't have tried it."

turkey

Two turkeys talking

turn

Turning to the left

turtle

Turtles turning to the right

twins

typewriter

Typing a letter

U u

umbrella

Uncle Uriah is
under his umbrella.

up

He is up on a pole.
He is upside down.

us

"He makes us laugh."

underwear

Uncle Uriah is in
his underwear.

use

"We use him for a horse."

V v

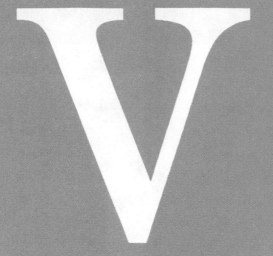

vacation

"We are going on our vacation."

vacuum

Vacuum cleaner

vaccination

valentine

From Uncle Uriah to Aunt Ada

120

valley

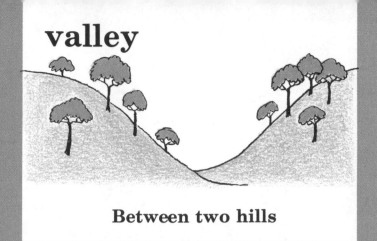

Between two hills

village

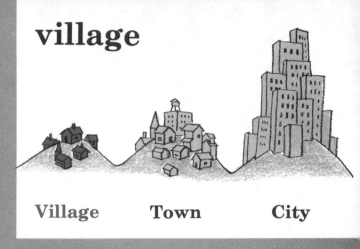

Village   **Town**   **City**

vanilla

Vanilla   **Strawberry**

violin

very

A very, very, very small dog

volcano

W W

wag

Wagging his tail

wait

"Wait! Wait! Wait for me!"

wagon

Wagging on a wagon

wake

She woke him up.

122

walk

Cats walking on a wall

walrus

A walrus
walking on a wall

warm

A walrus
trying to get warm

wash

Washing the baby

watch

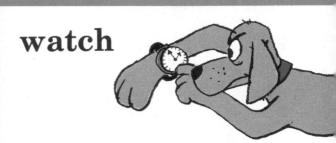

Watching a watch

water

Aunt Ada likes the water.
She is riding on a wave.

way

"Get out of my way."

123

wear

We are wearing green hats.

went

We went out in the rain.

week

Seven days

wet

We came home wet.

weigh

How much do we weigh?

whack

Mother was very angry.

whale

The biggest animal there is

wheel

Back wheel   **Front** wheel

which

Which twin is **which?**

whisker

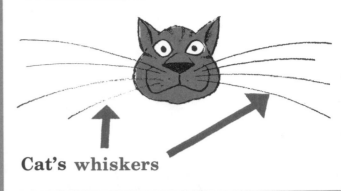

Cat's whiskers

whisper

A cat whispering

whistle

He comes when I whistle.

white

Black   **White**

why

He wants to know why.

wing

win

Who will win, the turtle or the rabbit?

wink

wind

The wind came in the window.

126

wipe

"Wipe your feet."

wish

"I wish I had a hot dog."

won't

"I won't eat it."

with
without

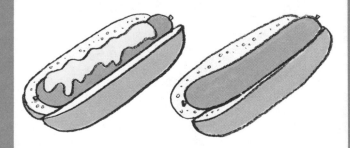

With **mustard** Without **mustard**

wood

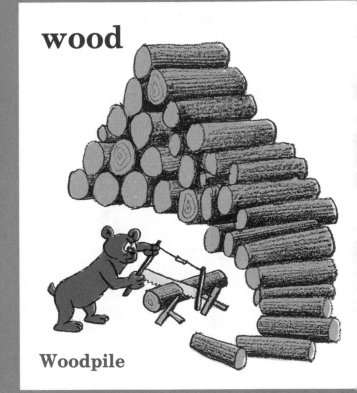

Woodpile

woman

One woman Three women

wool

"My wool is woolly."

127

word

Here are eight words. Do you know them all?

would
wouldn't

I wouldn't like to be a worm. Would you?

work

Hard work

write

I can write

world

Around the world

wrong

I KAN RITE

Aaron wrote it wrong.

xiphosuran

xanthochroid

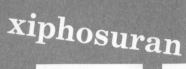
"Oh oh! X words are hard.."

xylophagous

xerophthalmia

"Don't worry. Here are three easy ones."

X

X

xanthophyll

Xmas

A short word for Christmas

x-ray

X-ray looks inside you.

xylophone

Y y

yard

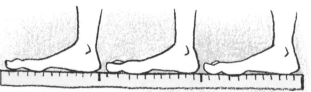

Three feet

yard

In our backyard
we have a hippopotamus.

yawn

Our hippopotamus
likes to yawn.

year

Twelve months

yell

I yell.   My dog yelps.

yellow

yes
yet

"Aren't you going to get up?"   "Yes, but not yet."

young

Young   Younger   Youngest

yoyo

Z z

zebras

zipper

"It's stuck.
I can't get out."

zoo

zero

Zero is very cold for zebras.